Dwell on the beauty of life.
Watch the stars, and see
yourself running with them.

Marcus Aurelius

THIS JOURNAL BELONGS TO

_____

_____

_____

TO: _____

FROM: _____

_____

_____

_____

_____

_____

_____

_____

_____

_____
_____
_____
_____
_____
_____
_____
_____
_____
_____
_____
_____
_____
_____
_____
_____
_____
_____
_____
_____
_____
_____
_____
_____
_____
_____

"You must find the place inside yourself
where nothing is impossible."

~ Deepak Chopra

"Always believe that something wonderful
is about to happen."

~ S. S. Dhillon

"Do what you can, with what you have,
where you are."

~ Theodore Roosevelt

_____
_____
_____
_____
_____
_____
_____
_____
_____
_____
_____
_____
_____
_____
_____
_____
_____
_____
_____
_____
_____
_____
_____
_____
_____
_____
_____
_____

"Wherever you go, go with all your heart."

~ Confucius

"You must be the change you wish
to see in the world."

~ Mahatma Gandhi

"Do not let the behavior of others
destroy your inner peace."

~ Dalai Lama

"A gem is not polished without rubbing,
nor a man perfected without trials."

~ Chinese Proverb

"The secret of happiness, you see, is not found in seeking more, but in developing the capacity to enjoy less."

~ Socrates

_____
_____
_____
_____
_____
_____
_____
_____
_____
_____
_____
_____
_____
_____
_____
_____
_____
_____
_____
_____
_____
_____
_____
_____
_____

"Defeat is always momentary."

~ Carl Denham (King Kong 2005)

"Every 'no' is a 'yes' to something."

~ Eric Micha'el Leventhal

_____

_____

_____

_____

_____

_____

_____

_____

_____

_____

_____

_____

_____

_____

_____

_____

_____

_____

_____

_____

_____

_____

_____

_____

_____

"Success is a lousy teacher. It seduces smart people
into thinking they can't lose."

~ Bill Gates

"Live as if you were to die tomorrow,
learn as if you were to live forever."

~ Mahatma Gandhi

_____

_____

_____

_____

_____

_____

_____

_____

_____

_____

_____

_____

_____

_____

_____

_____

_____

_____

_____

_____

_____

_____

_____

_____

_____

_____

_____

"It does not matter how slowly you go
as long as you do not stop."

~ Confucius

"Ask for what you want and be prepared to get it!"

~ Maya Angelou

_____

_____

_____

_____

_____

_____

_____

_____

_____

_____

_____

_____

_____

_____

_____

_____

_____

_____

_____

_____

_____

_____

_____

"Begin to live as though your prayers
are already answered."

~ Tony Robbins

"If you see it in your mind. You'll hold it in your hand."

~ Bob Proctor

"We are what we repeatedly do.
Excellence, then, is not an act, but a habit."

~ Aristotle

"Life shrinks or expands in proportion
to one's courage."

~ Anais Nin

_____

_____

_____

_____

_____

_____

_____

_____

_____

_____

_____

_____

_____

_____

_____

_____

_____

_____

_____

_____

_____

_____

"Change happens for you the moment you want
something more than you fear it."

~ Eric Micha'el Leventhal

"Experience is the teacher of all things."

~ Julius Caesar

"A journey of a thousand miles must begin
with a single step."

~ Lao Tzu

"I've failed over and over and over again
in my life and that is why I succeed."

~ Michael Jordan

_____

_____

_____

_____

_____

_____

_____

_____

_____

_____

_____

_____

_____

_____

_____

_____

_____

_____

_____

_____

_____

_____

_____

_____

_____

_____

"Our greatest glory is not in never failing,
but in rising every time we fall."

~ Confucius

"Life is like riding a bicycle. To keep your balance, you must keep moving."

~ Albert Einstein

_____

_____

_____

_____

_____

_____

_____

_____

_____

_____

_____

_____

_____

_____

_____

_____

_____

_____

_____

_____

_____

_____

_____

_____

"You have been assigned this mountain so that
you can show others it can be moved."

~ Mel Robbins (The 5 Second Rule)

"All great achievements require time."

~ Maya Angelou

"No matter how great the talent or efforts, some things take time. You can't produce a baby in one month by getting nine women pregnant."

~ Warren Buffett

_____

_____

_____

_____

_____

_____

_____

_____

_____

_____

_____

_____

_____

_____

_____

_____

_____

_____

_____

_____

_____

_____

_____

_____

"The only difference between a rich person and
poor person is how they use their time."

~ Robert Kiyosaki

"Try not to become a man of success but rather
to become a man of value."

~ Albert Einstein

"Life is a gift, and it offers us the privilege,
opportunity, and responsibility to give
something back by becoming more."

~ Tony Robbins

"Let us be grateful to the people who make us happy; they are the charming gardeners who make our souls blossom."

~ Marcel Proust

_____

_____

_____

_____

_____

_____

_____

_____

_____

_____

_____

_____

_____

_____

_____

_____

_____

_____

_____

_____

_____

_____

_____

_____

_____

"If you are planning for a year, sow rice;
if you are planning for a decade, plant trees;
if you are planning for a lifetime, educate people."

~ Chinese Proverb

"As we look ahead into the next century,
leaders will be those who empower others."

~ Bill Gates

"The best way to find yourself is to lose yourself
in the service of others."

~ Mahatma Gandhi

"Haters are a good problem to have. Nobody hates
the good ones. They hate the great ones."

~ Kobe Bryant

"There will always be someone who can't see
your worth. Don't let it be you."

~ Mel Robbins

"I can't give you a surefire formula for success,
but I can give you a formula for **failure**:
try to please everybody all the time."

~ Herbert Bayard Swope

_____

_____

_____

_____

_____

_____

_____

_____

_____

_____

_____

_____

_____

_____

_____

_____

_____

_____

_____

_____

_____

_____

_____

_____

_____

_____

"There is only one way to avoid criticism:
do nothing, say nothing, and be nothing."

~ Aristotle

"Leaders spend 5% of their time on the problem and 95% on the solution. Get over it and crush it!"

~ Tony Robbins

_____

_____

_____

_____

_____

_____

_____

_____

_____

_____

_____

_____

_____

_____

_____

_____

_____

_____

_____

_____

_____

_____

_____

_____

"The key is not to prioritize what's on your
schedule, but to schedule your priorities."

~ Stephen Covey

_____

_____

_____

_____

_____

_____

_____

_____

_____

_____

_____

_____

_____

_____

_____

_____

_____

_____

_____

_____

_____

_____

_____

"To know what people really think, pay regard to
what they **do** rather than what they **say**."

~ Rene Descartes

"Well done is better than well said."

~ Benjamin Franklin

"Seek first to understand, then to be understood."

~ Stephen Covey

"It's better to hang out with people better than you.
Pick out associates whose behavior is better than
yours and you'll drift in that direction."

~ Warren Buffett

"Do your own thinking independently.
Be the chess player, not the chess piece."

~ Ralph Charell

"It's not what you say out of your mouth
that determines your life, it's what you whisper
to yourself that has the most power!"

~ Robert Kiyosaki

"Your life is an expression of all your thoughts."

~ Marcus Aurelius

"Trade your expectation for appreciation
and the world changes instantly."

~ Tony Robbins

"Life is not a problem to be solved
but a reality to be experienced."

~ Soren Kierkegaard

"Breathe. Let go. And remind yourself that this very moment is the only one you know you have for sure."

~ Oprah Winfrey

_____

_____

_____

_____

_____

_____

_____

_____

_____

_____

_____

_____

_____

_____

_____

_____

_____

_____

_____

_____

_____

_____

"If you are depressed, you are living in the past.
If you are anxious, you are living in the future.
If you are at peace, you are living in the present."

~ Lao Tzu

"Life is really simple, but men insist
on making it complicated."

~ Confucius

"What we do now echoes in eternity."

~ Marcus Aurelius